The Little Book Of Successful Secrets

What Successful People Know, But Don't Talk About

JUSTIN PERRY & COSTAS SARRIS

ISBN: 1530466792
ISBN-13: 978-1530466795

CONTENTS

INTRODUCTION

Are you ready to create a life beyond your wildest dreams?

By the time you finish reading this book you will have gained the knowledge and power to create a life only a select few have been able to achieve.

I am able to say this, because this is exactly what I achieved for my life. With the knowledge found in this book, I was able to create a life that most people consider a fairytale. I earn over $360k every year through passive income, working from home. I go on at least 7 vacations to exotic places all over the world every year. I have a wonderful marriage with 3 beautiful children. I live in a half million dollar home (that is nearly paid off). I am a best selling author that has sold out in different countries. And, I am the CEO of the largest Self Help YouTube Channel, YouAreCreators. I did all of this using what most people call, "Law Of Attraction"

I bet this isn't the first time you've heard about the Law of Attraction...

You have probably seen the film 'The Secret' or maybe even read a book about it. You may have even experienced a few positive results after trying it out for yourself. But are you getting consistent results like some of the so called 'greats' who seem to succeed at everything they do?

These successful people all have one thing in common; they understand how to use the Law of Attraction.

Now I'm not saying that every successful person has studied the Law of Attraction, although many of them actually have (even ones that do not openly talk about it). But they are still successfully using the principles, whether they know it or not.

Here's the thing.

We are ALL using the Law of Attraction, every second, of every day, 100% of the time. It's not something you can turn on and off. It's a law of nature, just like gravity. The law of gravity is always pulling things towards the centre of the earth. The law of attraction is always pulling things towards you according to your thoughts, words, feelings and actions.

Some people are aware of this law and harness it to make their dreams come true while others, unfortunately, are unaware of this law and in turn use it to create lives of misery, poverty and sickness.

So what separates these two groups?

Their habitual thought patterns, feelings, actions and **Beliefs!**

I'm sure you have heard the Law of Attraction defined as "we attract what we think about", and it is true, but unless you have a good understanding of how to master your thoughts and emotions to become a **deliberate** creator of your life, it is unlikely you will be successful in using it.

I promise you that what you are about to learn will change your life forever, but only if you are willing to accept responsibility for your own life and commit to practicing these powerful principles like a samurai practices with his sword, each and every day.

I want to take a moment to emphasize the word PRACTICE. I remember when I first discovered the law of attraction, I just kept reading books and watching videos, never fully committing to practice the principles I learnt. I thought that by simply daydreaming about the life I wish I had I would attract it, which lead to 2 very long years of disappointment.

When I finally had enough of failing and decided to take real action, it was as if I unlocked the floodgates to everything I ever wanted. If it works for me, I know for a fact that it can also work for you.

Now say goodbye to your old, boring, mediocre life...

WHAT IS THE LAW OF ATTRACTION?

"You attract what you feel, what you are."

- **Denzel Washington**

Everything that is ever created starts in the mind as an idea.

EVERYTHING.

Every result is the product of a process that was started by a thought.

Your most dominant thoughts attract similar ideas, experiences and resources which eventually end up manifesting the idea in the physical world. You are like a living magnet that attracts and becomes what you think, feel, and say most often.

Allow thoughts of wealth to fill your mind all day long and you will start the process of wealth attraction. You will begin to feel inclined to take action and form relationships that are conducive to acquiring wealth. On the other hand, if you allow thoughts of lack and poverty to fill your mind all day long, you will cut off all opportunities that may move you in the direction of becoming wealthy, thus perpetuating a cycle of lack and poverty.

It sounds simple but it is not necessarily easy. You are going to have to form new habits of thoughts, feelings and actions. You will have to take the time to study and fully internalize the success principles presented to you in this book.

"If I want it, if I believe I can have it, then that's my reality. I'll attract it, it will attract to me."

- ***Big Sean (recording artist)***

Thoughts are a form of energy. Since the whole universe is made of this same energy, it is only logical to assume that our thoughts affect the universe and ultimately the physical reality we live in. Since everything is connected by this universal energy, the energy you put out affects the entire energy field on a subatomic level.

Think of thoughts as the air around us. They are both invisible to us but we know they are there. In order for air to affect physical reality, it must be intensely focused on a certain object, like a strong gust of wind on a tree. Same goes for your thoughts. In order to affect physical reality, your thoughts must be intensely focused on a particular outcome you wish to create. This strong collection of similar thoughts will in turn induce you to take the necessary action as well as attract all the resources and relationships needed to achieve this outcome.

When I first started writing this book, I wanted this part to explain why and how the Law of Attraction works the way it does using quantum physics and evidence from scientific experiments.

Then I realized that after many years of reading book after book and studying everything I could get my hands on, no-one actually knows **for sure** why the Law of Attraction exists and how it works. Science still cannot **fully** explain the law of gravity, magnetism or electricity. We just know they exist because we can observe their effects time after time.

One thing I do know for sure is that I have observed the effects of the Law of Attraction time after time in my own life and so have many other people. It's not necessary to understand **WHY** it works to reap the rewards, the same way you don't need to understand why electricity works to flick a light switch. But, just like electricity, this force can either be used constructively, like powering a light bulb, or destructively, as in the case of the electric chair.

It is called the **LAW** of attraction and just like all natural laws, it is always in full effect, no matter the circumstance. When a young child accidently walks off the edge of a cliff, gravity doesn't make an exception and suddenly stop operating because the child didn't know what they were doing. The same is true for the law of attraction. It doesn't stop operating just because someone is ignorant of the fact that their thoughts create their reality. Laws cannot think or decide what is right or wrong, they just are. It is our job to become aware of them and use them constructively.

"Whatever you're imagining you are attracting into your life."

- ***Redfoo (LMFAO)***

In this book we are going to study how you can consciously master this law to create the life you've always dreamed of.

It's obvious that people who have achieved great success are doing something right that others are not. That something different is how they habitually use their mind and focus. Your mind is more powerful than any supercomputer on the planet and by learning how to use it correctly you can achieve pretty much anything you want.

This is not a new discovery but it is also not very commonly known because many people either haven't taken the time to invest in themselves by learning what they need to know, are too lazy to apply the principles, or they simply don't want to change badly enough.

This book is giving you the key to success, but no-one else can use this key for you other than yourself. If you are prepared to commit to taking control of your own mind you can be, do, or have anything you want. You will finally understand the cause of success and how you can apply it in your own life.

"I am no longer cursed by poverty because I took possession of my own mind and that mind has yielded me every material thing I want, and much more than I need. But this power is a universal one, available to the humblest person as it is to the greatest."

- ***Andrew Carnegie***

CREATE YOUR VISION

"Just decide what it's going to be, who you're going to be, how you're going to do it. Just decide and then from that point the universe is going to get out of your way."

— **Will Smith**

The first step in creating a great life is deciding exactly what it is you want. Surprisingly very few people know **exactly** what they want from life. They just seem to go wherever their circumstances take them like a leaf blowing in the wind. The Law of Attraction is always at work in your life and is always giving you what you expect of it. The clearer you are about what you want, the more control you have over your life.

Up until now, your life has most likely been determined by the environmental conditioning you received from your parents, friends and teachers during your childhood. By creating a clear image of what you want from life you are deciding to control of your life instead of leaving it up to your past conditioning to determine what you will experience and become. You deserve and have every right to create an amazing life for yourself, but you first have to determine what that life looks like.

PURPOSE

I believe we are on earth for a purpose. To find this purpose, you have to follow the ideas and subjects that bring you the most happiness and fulfillment. Your purpose will always involve some sort of service to mankind. Coincidentally, serving is also how you build wealth for yourself. You see, your purpose will bring you everything you ever wanted. Happiness, success, wealth and abundance are all by-products of service to others. Give of yourself; give your talents, gifts, and time, and the outcome will be more glorious then you can ever imagine. You receive first by giving.

Who do you want to be? How do you want to live? What do you want to have, experience and contribute during your lifetime? You have to get really **clear** on this vision, describe it with as much detail as you possibly can, for all areas of your life. Make this vision so compelling that it **pulls** you towards it. Go as big as you want, there are **no limits**.

Don't worry about being realistic, as long as it is possible for a human to achieve (unfortunately you can't expect to grow wings and fly, a private jet will have to do...if that's what you want...). Write this vision down in detail so you can use it in your visualization which I'll get to in a bit.

Here's how to find your purpose. Ask yourself, "What do I love doing that brings me intense happiness"? What am I naturally good at? What was the one thing that people always told me I was really good at? What is the thing I would do for free even if I didn't have to? Listen to your intuition and follow those leads. Those leads will lead you to your life's purpose and passion. Anything connected to your purpose has to flourish, because passion is connected to it.

"I believe that when you know where you're going and you know what you want the universe has a way of stepping aside for you."

- Jon 'Bones' Jones (UFC Champion)

PAIN (PUSH) & PLEASURE (PULL)

As well as having a vision that pulls you towards it, it is equally important to have something pushing you from behind too. Many times people create a compelling vision for themselves but at the same time they feel too comfortable with their current situation to face the fear of moving outside their comfort zone to achieve their vision.

You need to transform this fear into a constructive force that helps **push** you towards your vision. You do this by getting clear on all the reasons why you refuse to carry on living your current circumstances and essentially a quality of life that is less than your ultimate vision and what you deserve.

This is one thing that many people who reach the heights of great success have in common. They have experienced really tough times in their lives and have made a decision to never experience that pain again. This is where their drive comes from and you need to create the same driving force in **your** life.

Hitting rock bottom isn't necessarily a bad thing. Sometimes it can be used as a trampoline, propelling you to inconceivable heights. I remember when I hit rock bottom. I was 23 years old, $43 in the bank, with a wife and two kids. I had just been laid off and had recently failed out of Fire School (During the last day of school!). I had no hope, no guidance, and no money. I went through this mental rough patch for about a year, and during that year, I attracted every negative situation you can think of. I was pitiful. It wasn't until I hit rock bottom that I began to seek out a better life. I was sick and tired of being sick and tired. When I made up my mind that I wasn't going to live like this anymore, I started to attract everything I needed to change my life. That was when a successful friend of mine introduced me to the Law Of Attraction.

Associate **pain** to not achieving your vision, get angry about it. Anger is good when it is used to drive you towards bigger, better things. What disgusts you about your current situation? What do you refuse to carry on putting up with? List as many things as you can.

Then choose to associate **pleasure** with achieving your vision. How good does it feel to jump out of bed in the morning because your life is just so exciting? How many lives are improved because of your success? Who has been inspired by seeing you achieve all these great things? List all the reasons why achieving your vision is a good thing.

This creates a dual push and pull force, propelling you to your success instead of two conflicting forces working against each other.

GOALS

"Dreams without goals remain dreams and ultimately fuel disappointment."

- **Denzel Washington**

The next step is to turn your vision into long term goals. This provides your subconscious mind with multiple clear targets on which to focus and start using its powerful resources to move you towards. Clear, compelling goals act like magnets, pulling you towards them.

Write out the end result for each area of your life in your vision as if you have already achieved it. Stating your goals as if they are a present fact is crucial in using the Law of Attraction successfully. It is important to write a clear list of goals because part of your new daily routine will be to read these goals every morning and every night. Your subconscious mind takes your thoughts and words literally, so it is important to state your goals in the present tense. If you state your goals as something that will happen in the future, your subconscious will keep creating situations where your goals are stuck in the future.

"You have to create a goal for yourself, whatever that may be, a short-term goal and a long-term goal and you have to go after that. If you do not see it and if you do not believe it, who else will?"

- **Arnold Schwarzenegger**

Now break down each of these long-term goals into short-term goals. Decide what you expect to achieve in the next ninety days. I'm guessing your ultimate long-term goals are big enough that you cannot expect to reach them in ninety days. Setting short-term goals gives you manageable targets to aim for that you can start taking action on right away. They will help create momentum towards your vision while at the same time not overwhelming you.

If your long-term goals CAN be achieved in ninety days you are probably underestimating your potential and selling yourself short. If you fail to dream big enough you are depriving yourself and the world of the gifts you have to offer. Don't limit yourself. Be fearless, dream big and go for it!

VISION BOARD

If you are a visual person you can even create a vision board. Collect photos that represent different aspects of your ultimate vision that will motivate you every time you see them. You can create your vision board either physically or digitally. Place it somewhere it will be seen regularly to act as a reminder and source of inspiration. You can even change the desktop image to your computer to match the things you desire. Or you can change the front image or background of your Cell phone to display your goals or material objects. Remember, what you focus on the longest grows the strongest!

"I think that there's a certain delusional quality that all successful people have to have."

- ***Will Smith***

Every time you look at your vision board, take a few seconds to visualize and feel what it would feel like if you were already in possession of the objects. Close your eyes and visualize using or having every item on your vision board. Feel as if it's already in your possession. This helps you vibrate at the same frequency, which creates a strong magnetic force between you and your goals.

VISUALIZATION

"I'm a very driven, ambitious person. But I'm a spiritual person as well. I believe in creative visualization."

- **Victoria Beckham**

Visualization is the most effective way to communicate a target to your subconscious mind. Regular visualization will be your most powerful tool in turning your vision into reality. It's the images you hold in your mind that inspire your actions and attract your visions. The more you practice seeing yourself as being successful, the more you will take action and attract people, resources and circumstances that are congruent with your successful self-image.

Visualization is something we all do. Daydreaming is unfocused visualization. The trick is to learn to daydream in a disciplined manner which is focused on the goals you wish to achieve. Not everyone sees vivid imagery when they visualize, some people are more auditory and so they hear conversations and sounds of a certain scene. Others and more kinesthetic and they feel the movement and physical interaction of a scene. There is no right or wrong way to visualize, as long as you are doing what is natural to you when attempting to imagine a future goal as a present reality.

WHEN TO VISUALIZE

The best times to visualize are when you wake up in the morning and before you go to bed at night. This is when your body is most relaxed and your subconscious mind is most receptive to suggestion. However you can visualize any time of the day just as effectively if you relax right before you start. Visualizing before you go to sleep has the added bonus of allowing your subconscious mind to work on the images of your goals while you sleep by using your dreams as a tool to create plans for the achievement of your goals.

"This is the Law of Attraction... When things are going good and you visualize more good things happening that's easy. What's not easy to do is when things are going bad and you're visualizing the good stuff, and that is what I was able to do. Even though I was having these troubles at home, even though I had no job, no security...I still was able to feel like it was, like a kid would use his imagination."

- *Conor McGregor (UFC Champion)*

Alternatively, you can visualize whenever you have some downtime. If you're waiting in line at the bank, you can use this time to visualize and feel the emotions of walking up to the bank teller and cashing a check for a million dollars. If you're at a bar waiting to be served, visualize meeting your ideal partner and hitting it off. The possibilities and applications of visualization are endless. Get creative and experiment with new ideas until it becomes second nature.

Also, don't force your visualizations. Let the image of your desired state pop in your mind's eye, and allow infinite intelligence to fill the details. We're co-creating our reality with a force that knows exactly what it's doing, trust the process...

RELAXATION

If you are able to, it is much more powerful to visualize in a deep state of relaxation. For example, in the morning when you wake up and before you go to bed, it would be a good idea to use this simple technique to relax so you can get the most out of your visualization practice.

Lie or sit in a comfortable position and close your eyes. Now, consciously relax each body part one-by-one, starting from your head, moving all the way down to your arms and your feet. You can simply repeat "My _____ is now relaxed" for each body part while feeling and allowing each one completely relax and release all tension. Then simply count down from 10 to 1, feeling yourself go into a deeper and deeper state of relaxation. You will now find yourself in a very relaxed state. Your brain waves will be operating in the Theta state which is the most powerful and effective frequency for visualization and making suggestions to your subconscious mind.

HOW TO VISUALIZE

You can now start to visualize yourself being and doing whatever you would be doing if your vision were already true. There are two main types of visualization you can use. You can either imagine sitting in your own private cinema, watching yourself on the screen. This is called disassociated visualization. The second type is called associated visualization. This is where you experience everything in first person by visualizing from your own point of view within the vision. Experiment with both to see what works best for you. I suggest you use both methods, starting off with disassociated visualization and then jumping into your body to experience it as an associated visualization.

"Imagination is everything. It is the preview of life's coming attractions."

- ***Albert Einstein***

Include as many of the five senses and details as you can when visualizing. The more details, the greater the force of attraction. What does that new car smell like? What do the dials look like on the dashboard? How good does your favorite music sound coming through the speakers?

Don't worry if the images you are visualizing are not crystal clear. What is important is that you allow yourself to experience the vision as if it is already happening **right now** so that you **feel** the same feelings you would if it were **already true**. It is this feeling of strong emotion associated with your vision that communicates to your subconscious that the goal you are visualizing is already a present fact.

Your subconscious has no concept of time. It also does not know the difference between the real world and the imagined world. Your body and nervous system react to your imagination as if it were really happening right now. If you don't believe me close your eyes for a moment and imagine biting into a juicy lemon. Notice how you start to salivate and are able to smell and taste the lemon. This is just one example of how suggestible your subconscious is to your imagination.

"Imagine you had everything you ever wanted, everything. Imagine you were everything you ever wanted to be. Encapture that feeling. That's the easiest way to manifest what you want."

- ***Big Sean (Recording Artist)***

MENTAL REHEARSAL

There is one famous study where a group of basketball players were split into three groups. The first group practiced their free throws every day for 20 days. The second group didn't practice at all for 20 days. The third group only practiced successfully shooting free throws in their imagination for 20 minutes a day for 20 days. They were all scored before and after the 20 days. The results were clear. The group that had no practice made no improvement. However the group that practiced with a real ball improved 24% and the group that practiced only in their imaginations improved 23%!

The players who practiced in their imaginations were activating their nervous system every time they visualized shooting a free throw. This mental practice conditioned their nervous system with what a successful free throw feels like and when it came to taking a real shot their body responded the same way it did during the visualization.

"I'm gonna go and think and I'm gonna vision myself tearing this (concert) down. That's how you do it, you have to vision it first."

- ***Jay Z (Recording Artist)***

SELF IMAGE

In the book 'Psycho-Cybernetics' (which I highly recommend) it says:

"When you see a thing clearly in your mind, your creative 'success mechanism' within you takes over and does the job much better than you could do it by conscious effort or willpower."

Maxwell Maltz, the author of Psycho-Cybernetics, was a plastic surgeon who noticed it wasn't peoples outer appearances that made them feel better or worse, more or less successful, it was their self-image.

The main premise of that book was to help us understand, we all have a self-image that controls what we can and cannot accomplish, what is difficult or what is easy, even how others respond to us. All your actions, feelings, behaviors and abilities are always consistent with your self-image.

He started to tell people that, before he would agree to give them plastic surgery, they should visit their 'theatre of the mind' (imagination) daily for 30 minutes and see themselves as they wish to be. Soon many of the people practicing this were displaying better results in their lives than the people who underwent plastic surgery.

This was when he discovered the power of the visualization. He spent the rest of his life dedicated to researching the effects of the "success mechanism" on many different people in all walks of life: athletes, coaches, salesman, CEO's, actors, poor people, sick people, people with anxiety ...

He noticed miraculous improvements in the lives of all these people when they changed their self-image. The main techniques he used were the daily 'theatre of the mind' practice and goal setting. He believed that the common trait among people who were fulfilled in their lives was that they all had goals they were striving for which gave their life purpose.

By practicing the achievement of their goals in their 'theatre of the mind' they were able to accomplish them faster, more effectively and with more ease.

"The mind is really so incredible. Before I won my first Mr. Universe title, I walked around the tournament like I owned it. I had won it so many times in my mind, the title was already mine. Then when I moved on to the movies I used the same technique. I visualized daily being a successful actor and earning big money."

- Arnold Schwarzenegger

WEALTH

For the rich to become rich, they had to become comfortable with the idea of becoming wealthy. Most people have a sneaky subconscious guilt about wanting to be rich and prosperous. That subconscious guilt is exactly what blocks your avenues of wealth and abundance.

We have to understand on a deep subconscious level, that wealth and prosperity is our birthright, and that there is more than enough for everyone. The universe is superfluous in its giving, we are always provided for. The only way for you to pinch yourself off from the flow of abundance, is to believe that there is a lack of abundance, which is called "scarcity thinking".

The universe organizes itself according to our beliefs, so if we believe in scarcity and lack, that is exactly what is projected in our life. I went from making 20k a year doing something I absolutely hated, to making over 360K a year doing something I absolutely love. Once I became comfortable with the belief that I deserve prosperity and abundance, ideas of wealth flooded my mind, and I began to act on them. You can do the same, but I takes a committed effort.

"Whatever you hold in your mind on a consistent basis is exactly what you will experience in your life."

- **Tony Robbins**

You're probably asking how I became comfortable with the idea of attaining wealth? I became comfortable by constantly drilling the thoughts of wealth into my mind. I would sleep with wealth affirmations playing on repeat (in a low comfortable volume). I would visualize myself already in a wealthy state. I would play make believe with my wife, and act as if we were already prosperous. We completely changed our vocabulary in regards to wealth. In the past we would say, "I don't have any money", but we changed that to, "I am always prosperous, I always have an abundance of money." My positive thoughts about money became my dominant thoughts about money, thus eliminating negative ones, and tipping the scale of prosperity.

Your imagination is your power to create, so use it wisely. Do you use it to imagine success or failure? Make a commitment to discipline your imagination and banish any scenes of failure you have been rehearsing. Instead, choose to create "mind movies" of great health, wealth, success, love and happiness. Refine the details of this movie every day and watch it play on repeat in the 'theatre of the mind'.

"The man who has no imagination has no wings."

- ***Muhammad Ali***

TAKE ACTION

Oprah Winfrey: *"Visualization works if you work hard."*

Jim Carrey: *"Well yeah, that's the thing. You can't just visualize and then go eat a sandwich."*

A common misconception people make when it comes to the Law of Attraction is that visualization replaces action. These are the same people that sit at home, visualize about being successful for five minutes and then complain the next day when nothing comes of it. Faith without works (action) is completely dead!

Goal setting and visualization are important but that is only half the work. By doing this you have placed your order for your vision, and the universe will set up all the necessary components for its achievement. You must then take all the necessary **action** to claim your order.

The process of visualization does not invalidate the value of action. It is a tool that is used to focus our actions and communicate with universal intelligence in order to increase the effectiveness of our actions in achieving our goals. If you have a garden full of weeds, you cannot simply repeat the affirmation "there are no weeds, there are no weeds, there are no weeds" and expect the weeds to disappear the next day. Instead, you must visualize your garden without any weeds and then proceed to take action in removing these weeds until your garden matches the vision in your head. The vision is the blueprint and the actions are what bring this blueprint to life.

Don't just take any action, but take **inspired** action. When you feel led to call someone, or go someplace, FOLLOW THOSE LEADS! Many successful businessmen and women say that they follow their gut more than anything. They attribute their success to the guidance of their intuition. Your intuition or "gut feeling", is infinite intelligence instructing you where and when to act. Never ignore your leads!

DAILY ACTION

If you visualize your goals but then go back to living a life of laziness and complacency you are basically saying that you do not really believe in your vision or that your desire to manifest this vision is not strong enough.

You have to live with the faith that you are destined for your vision, not just when you sit down to visualize it but all day long, in everything that you do! It should permeate every action you take because you know that each action is moving you one step closer to your dream life.

Wallace Wattles, in his book 'The Science of Getting Rich', says the most important part in using this universal law of attraction is to do all that can be done each day. Take massive action towards your goals, daily. This builds strong momentum and makes it easier to continue taking action every day.

There is a Japanese philosophy, *kaizen*, that is the practice of continuous small improvement in order to achieve greatness. Daily actions, no matter how small, compound and create massive long-term results. Commit to this principle of kaizen and start taking action everyday towards your goals. You will be amazed at what can be achieved in as little as 90 days with this kind of consistency in action.

BE HONEST WITH YOURSELF

"Don't be afraid to close your eyes and dream, but then open your eyes and see...The only way forward is to be real about what it's going to take to achieve those dreams. You have to be honest with yourself"

- **Sean 'Diddy' Combs**

It is going to take as much work as you **believe** it will take. Your beliefs govern your reality. This is why it is important to be honest with yourself about what you **really** believe it's going to take to make your ultimate vision come true.

Visualizing a clear target allows your 'success mechanism' to put the pieces together and calculate a clear path for you to take, however you will have to walk that path.

If you keep lying to yourself about what needs to be done because you are too lazy to act on it, then you have no right to complain if you fall short of your goals. You must be willing to do whatever it takes to make your dreams come true and if you are honest with yourself, you will know exactly what needs to be done.

FEEL & ACT AS-IF

The best way to stay on track towards your vision is to really become familiar with the feeling and the perspective you have when you visualize yourself already living your ultimate vision. The more you practice visualizing the end goal, the more familiar the feeling becomes.

Moving through life with this new perspective, you will start to become aware of new opportunities as well as ones that were always there but you didn't notice from your old perspective. When you take action with this new self-image you will have clarity on what it is you need to do at all times to keep moving towards your vision.

Another great way to act as-if is to celebrate as-if you have finally achieved all your goals and dreams. Take a couple minutes to really celebrate, pump your fists in the air, jump around, play some party music and bask in the feeling of success. This is a very powerful technique to acquire a success consciousness and develop the self-image of a winner. Use your imagination like a child would, to create the sense of achievement.

If you feel successful (consistently), your reality will soon reflect that success. Guaranteed.

DEFEAT YOUR DOUBT

"Before I learned about the Law of Attraction I was aware of the power of my thoughts, staying focussed, weeding out thoughts that sabotage."

- Jay Z

If you ever have old negative thoughts showing up trying to discourage you, simply look back at your goals and focus on them. Regain the perspective of that successful version of yourself from your vision. This is why it was important to create a clear vision that is so compelling it pulls you towards it. When your desire is greater than your fears, you are sure to blast through that fear to reach your goals. Just reframe any fear you feel as excitement, it's the same feeling just a different label. This empowers you to use it as a force for positive action instead of allowing it to hold you back.

"Believe nothing, no matter where you read it or who has said it, not even if I have said it, unless it agrees with your own reason and your own common sense."

- Buddha

The only enemy of man is doubt and fear. The funny part is, fear isn't even real. Think about it. When you're fearful, you're nervously apprehensive of an outcome that hasn't even occurred yet. Basically, you're afraid of something "might" going wrong. You have to realize, how powerful your "focus" is. What we consciously focus on, we draw into our reality. Quantum physics proves, that by merely observing electrons (the stuff everything is made of), we bring them into this solid dimension. The same goes in the mental world. What we focus on or observe, we make real. Since we know this, it would behove you focus solely on the things you want to happen rather than the things you don't. Consciously choose! If you are in doubt, then switch your thoughts to one of confidence and assurance. If you are feeling fearful, switch to thoughts of boldness and supreme faith. The more you are able to switch these thoughts from negative to positive, the more control you'll have over your success.

Rational thinking can also be used as a tool to overcome fear. Use your rational thinking to decide if something doesn't make sense by having an internal debate on the subject, arguing both for and against the topic until you come to a clear resolution on what you believe to be the truth. Once you come to a clear conclusion, argue for your new point of view with so much emotional intensity and conviction that the new belief has now overwritten the old one.

EMPOWERING QUESTIONS

"Quality questions create a quality life. Successful people ask better questions, and as a result, get better answers."

-   Tony Robbins

Empowering questions are also a great and powerful tool to have at your disposal on your journey to success. Your mind works like an internal super-computer that always provides an affirming answer to the questions you ask it.

For example, if you ask "Why am I always broke?" then it will manufacture an answer affirming why you're always broke, such as "Because you're too lazy and lack self confidence". Your brain will provide the correct answer and it will make sense to you in that moment. The problem with this is that the question is setting you up for disappointment. It is **assuming** that you will always be lazy and lack confidence.

A better question would be "How am I going to earn $10,000 a month doing something I love?" This immediately shifts your focus towards a positive outcome and your internal super-computer will start to give you more empowering and useful answers. Get into the habit of controlling your mind and focus by using empowering questions in everything you do. This is a common trait of happy, successful people. They are always asking themselves high quality questions which lead to high quality answers and ultimately a high quality life.

AFFIRMATIONS

Affirmations are words or phrases that are said over and over with the intention of impressing the subconscious mind. I suggest as part of your daily practice that you read your goals as affirmations every morning when you wake up and every night before bed. After reading each goal take a minute to close your eyes, and visualize and feel it as-if it is already real before moving onto the next one.

This simple exercise will take no longer than 10 minutes but it has the power to completely change the course of your life. I challenge you to stick to this life changing habit for at least 30 days. You will be amazed by the shifts you will experience in your mind-set and actions.

"Create a vision of who you want to be and then live into that picture as if it were already true."

*- **Arnold Schwarzenegger***

THE WRAP UP

You now have all the tools you need to create a life of great health, wealth and happiness. It is up to you to accept responsibility and put these tools to use in your own life.

Create your ultimate vision.

Visualize it daily and assume the feeling that you've already achieved it.

Commit to taking action this very moment to make all your dreams come true instead of pretending you don't have what it takes!

Refuse to live another day with the illusion that you are powerless to life's circumstances. You really do have a deep reservoir of power within you. It is eagerly awaiting your command so it can assist you in creating the great life you deserve.

YOU ARE POWERFUL! Never forget that.

We hope that you have found this book to be enlightening and fulfilling. You'll also realize that there's a part of you that has always known this information. We are thrilled to have been the tools that have sparked your memory. Now go and create the marvelous lives you most earnestly deserve.

Check out our YouTube channels **VYBO** and **YouAreCreators** for more amazing content on personal development and the law of attraction.

Finally, if you enjoyed this book, we would really appreciate it if you could take 10 seconds to leave a review (on Amazon or any sales platform the book was purchased on) . It will help us reach others with this valuable information as well as allow us to continue creating content that inspires and empowers people to live amazing lives!

Thank you and good luck! (You won't need it)

www.VYBO.co

www.YouAreCreators.org